# Connemara

Keith MacNider

# Connemara Greening

# Acknowledgements

Keith MacNider's writings have been previously published in the
following magazines and literary journals:
*The Antagonish Review*, Canada
*Blue Heron Review,* USA
*Earth Mother*, SA
*Fleurieu Past & Present*, SA
*Friendly Street Readers*, SA
*Mascara Review*, NSW
*Spectrum*, Middleton Writers Anthology, SA
*Milang Community News*, SA
*Milang Station: Railway Poems*, SA
*Psychosynthesis Journal*, SA
*The Nature of Poetry: an experience of the Four Directions
from Canyon de Chelly*, USA
*Speak Out*: Sand Writers anthologies, SA
*Southern Echoes: an anthology of Druid Writing*, WA
*Thin Air – Arts & Words*, SA
*Tamba*, Vic
*Touchstone: the journal of the Order of Bards, Ovates & Druids*, UK

First published 2022 by
**GINNINDERRA PRESS**
PO Box 3461 Port Adelaide 5015
www.ginninderrapress.com.au

# Contents

# Preface

These poems come from a long way back, born of my family of origin and the countries I've lived in: England, Hong Kong, Australia, also those that I've spent considerable time in. I was inspired by participating in Kim Rosen's Poetry Depths Mystery Schools in Ireland, and John Fox's Nature of Poetry workshops in the Navaho Reservation in Chinle, Arizona, as well as a poetry workshop on Molokai, Hawaii.

I also participated in workshops and programmes run by the late and great English poet Jay Ramsay in England. He and I thought of each other as brothers – and his influence remains as a love of words, and the deep love of the land.

I give thanks to my fellow writers in Sand Writers, based in Goolwa, South Australia: a great and fun group where sharing writing is a rich experience.

This poetry collection would not have been possible without the bounteous love and generosity of Dorrie MacNider, the friendship of Professor Roger Rees and Peter Strahan, and the abiding friendship and acumen of South Australia's award-winning poet and editor, Jude Aquilina. Jude encouraged me throughout the whole process of writing and shaping this manuscript. Her Milang Poets series had a big impact on me, broadening my writing.

I give thanks too to Stephen Matthews and Ginninderra Press for accepting my manuscript for publication, and for finally bringing a young teen's dream of being published to fruition. I am glad that the me of that time knew instinctively that one day I would be a writer of words that would be born of the heart and of the land.

Accordingly, I am grateful for the many literary journals that have accepted my poems over the years. And I acknowledge the work and writing of Mari-Jo Moore, author of *Genocide of the Mind*, for our sharing of ideas.

Keith MacNider

# Place Song

What are those places you don't know
yet which know you before you arrive?
Perhaps they've been waiting unadorned
and barely noticeable in your readings
and yet like sunrise they reshape who
you are, the way a mountain shedding grief
returns to song and you wait at the base
gathering notes from the sun and moon.
Is it then the first breakthrough, first steps home?

# Connemara Greening

His prose, thickened from small shoot to trunk,
as if woven by the wind and tiny sprites that
walked the path each night when the moon was dulling
and the sea answered his questions with that wish wash
sound it murmured against the nearby shore. Perhaps
each night his words became prayers as they slipped
into the dark? Perhaps they were never meant to be
but became so, black and tipped with indefatigable
light? I know when I read them I think of the rain-sodden
paths, the bogs that hold the light even on
the darkest days, stones that seem to chat and chant,
mists that beard the mountains, swaths of ferns
rippling like green freckled velvet, that something
far older is present, an ancient pathway like a band of
light around which words begin to coalesce, something
you can't see but feel in your bones, a hum,
a honing of sight.

# Wending

Just when you think you've got
it all figured something else
stands out and you've got to get
back to the first brush stroke
and begin again from that which
called you. Only then in the indentation
comes the first surprise that knew
you before it. It's then the red
mountains and stones begin to paint
you as you them, that they remind
you of your first decision to sketch
those years ago, a gentleness
like an unseen river quietly heard.

# Mountain Light Drops

Like pinched water veins,
silhouettes of themselves.

You smile as if stung by curves
sharper than your own.

I can't wait and turn to walk
back past the future you once
promised.

I don't have the keys and the car
is gone, stolen by the clouds.

## The Lone Beach

He washes up on a beach of his own
longing, unsteady and tired, as if all
he wanted was just out of reach
and yet floats by, like a language
lost and about to be found.

# Walking Between

I've been out for a walk, looking between the trees
for something that would remind me of your footsteps.
Perhaps I'm too early and you're still home, washing
your stones that they may shine in freedom, and you'll
smile that faraway smile that's like a boat to an elsewhere
intrinsically yours. What it is to look out from the point,
the way the sea surges and quietens, surges again.
and you'd chant, the sea singing you, you the rocks
and their collaboration with the earth and sky, reaching
up and holding still, how contradictions sculpted
your pathways, original, I rich with yearning?

# Verge Green

She said he dreamt in green, various shades of it,
that he thought it kept him alive, a promise of
the green hills of his birth, of stretching in the sun,
wild dives into the sea, its blue-green waters,
of standing wave tipped, that sense of being
on the verge of things, an elsewhere close
and faraway, a different stream of ideas
that he heard again when drumming,
his heart a mouthpiece, his words a clan,
a tartan fold, and she dancing with him,
steps beyond steps, a rock face choir
that she sings with, as quiet as the stars.

# Leaving

So he's left wandering
through the gap of his
own making, as if that were the only way
he could make sense now, rainbow
on the edge of the sky, music trailing,
the one fire ahead, his small toe broken,
his limp pressing into the earth,
and she on the hillside
counting the steps to revival,
a mist the first whisper,
a silent quiver in the meaning of yesterday.

# Moments of Sky

Moments when hands don't reach
and presence is measured in absence,
he with the first reminder of what
it took to slip away and let the ocean
hold him, head just above water,
ideas afloat but inviting other, stars
resting on the hilltop, memories
of his first car, the swing up into
the mountains, the frost making
for edginess, and she next to him
leaning into the future even as she
spoke about the past, conversational
and ready to ride the clouds, a sky-farer,
and he the cartographer of all she desired.

## Moon Silt

The moon's light visits us this evening.
We feel a presence like the silt of an
ancient cave and yet lightening so that
we both smile and sigh at much the
same time. Even the dog looks up
as if poised on the edge of discovery.
Perhaps the axis of our relationship
is moving, tilting into another, closer
phase, a swimming under the surface
of a Minoan pool, greened and rippling.

# Beeches

Where are you when I look for you amongst the beeches,
trees that always seemed to call you home to yourself,
an elegance born of the green tipped desire to be whole?

Is it you who has become tidal, drawn to the small inlets,
profuse and damp? Even when it was cold you'd
walk barefoot, the sand comforting, sometimes so smooth

but mostly grainy, always inviting the dip into the water, even
on the coldest days, shouting like a child, exuberant
and filled with the deep, contradictory ways of life,

your life. Perhaps one day a canoe came for you,
as if undeniably yours, and words became less
than more and silence gathered you up

and the beech tree loosened its grip of you
and you became whatever else was calling you,
DNA you'd say, DNA.

# A Celtic Bracelet of Eye

The crane gives up the fish.
Silvery, alive, it calls forth eye.

It is a precious gift.

See that this fish is well looked after,
and yet take of it that it be re-born,

for to deny the life of the fish immortal,
is to deny the life within.

Sparkle like a silvery bracelet of eye.

# Where the Trees Dance

The old voices gather
as if wrapped in long grass,
the winter's pleasure.

Some days when the sky
thickens and the breeze
sings you can hear the old

paths re-emerge, moving
into place, and you have
to get out of your car

and dance something
very old, budding new.

# What Song the Other?

I've come to a place that sings.
Perhaps it's the sky looking
at the land and the earth smiling
at its good fortune to be heard.

I know that when he walked
the vast open spaces of his
yearning he found flowers
in the quietest of places

small nooks in-between
rocks or stretching over
the earth as if nothing
would ever contain them.

# Green Sway

Those stones sung into song by the early morning light as if nothing else were happening but this sensual touch of air and stones and your own dreaming. What then to be one of a number, constellations of joy and regret, the moving pieces of an orchestra you can't see but feel within, as if chosen by stones their green ridges and flat plains, like a canoe of recovering, buoyant with hope?

# She Braided Words

She braided words the way the river
puckered into smiles when the wind
blew hard.

So too her words emerged from the deep,
laced with song, curved like the river's
bends, she her eyes closed, listening

to the rocks and hollows where no sounds
swam, and yet even there she could trace
the lineage of beginnings.

## Stone Touch

Each time I touch you,
a green stone flecked with grey
I hear something of water
the way it pools where
the mountain levels
as if holding its breath,
and then gathers pace
chattering with sudden
gushing rain. Maybe
I am in one of those moments
freckled with desire, the sun
rising, the loch waiting
for all that is and isn't
and I am aligned with Jupiter
and travel is in the cards,
the stone a canoe, heart a messenger.

# Amber

In the forested eye
you rich and resinous
amber streaming with light.

And when you sleep,
curled up in the curve
of the new moon,

your body quivers
and twitches, ever so slight
movements as if travelling

between the worlds, the way
the forest breathes in light
and gives out life.

# Where Rock Sees Sky

I lean against the granite boulder,
its orange lichen comforting, edging
against my bare back.
It's cool but sunny, a musical
score of breeze, sea air, heated
remains of the deep past.

Perhaps it is an ancient grandparent
to my gaze, born of tumultuous waves,
memories of the Earth, witness to
shipwrecks, invasion, embedded
understandings of the original
peoples, the way the heart knows

before the mind, day curling into
evening, the dog moving me
into walking, the return trail,
the beginning eye that remembers
without having to.

# Today the Tiny Silvery Brown Snake

as eager to be alive as the dawn,
silent and shimmering its way
across the path as if a song
were to be born when its belly
would be full

and us with our feet moving right
near it, stopping to let it go, and it
too pausing as if to listen to our own
vibrations,

the way thought reaches out and has a tone –
a quiver – that tells each of us it's alright
to stop and dwell just that while before
we all move again and the day
curves into other meaning.

# Trails

So many trails, the mountain an eye,
his steps even, paced by will, the familiar
and the yet to be, edging into other,
places that talk through cracks in resolve,
in the smallest of ways that seem so much
more than he knew, and he'd nod to that,
the knowing and the not, gaps where the light
fell, where insistence had no point, just the
flickering of doubt, surrender to the heart,
a hearth in the making in the very effort
not to make, but to be, open and listening.

# He Waits By the Gate

checking his phone,
seeking her messages,
arrangements and all
that still waits, thinks of
that first flurry of attraction,
deep attention, when everything
was important and so much
else wasn't.

He looks at the sky, the swirl
of clouds, rain further away,
the day closing on cold. He
hears the tide rustling in the bay
close by, little murmurs,
omens and sayings, return
of doubt, she her red hair,
those deep blue eyes,
like a yacht running
the sea, so many things
gathered in his pocket,
timeless and not, places
that recur, rebound,
filling the silence, and yet
silence itself. He puts
the phone in his pocket,
walks away, each step
a reminder, each step not.

# Thimbled Eye

She pats the dog, ruffles its hair, plucks
out a small prickle, another two, her voice
gentle, hand patting the dog.

The day murmurs past two. Time,
so often elsewhere, is close. She cleans
her spectacles though she doesn't call them that.

That is an elsewhere that perhaps
the cats she once had, knew. She
was younger then.

It's evening and she draws the curtains,
sits down and gets out a dictionary,

traces the etymology of a word or two,
perhaps more. These days that is how

she travels, into the origins of words,
their sounds, the history of living.

Lately she has started learning Swedish,
edging into different tones, learns

to let go of having to master the language
takes on being bold no matter what
she might do.

# Mountain Seer

He took himself up the mountain, exercise
and a view across to the islands, the three
of them covered in a foggy haze.

Sometimes there he'd hear music and songs
as if born of the ancients, words he got close to
but stopped at trying to be exact,

for these moments were like a patchwork
field where stone walls might sing or a horse
white and supple might straddle the sea.

Those days he wrote down what he could
and left empty spaces that the wind might
greet, or a cloud whisper close to him

and he'd know he was alive and life was well.

# Arctic Journey

She said those mountains dreamed you
when you woke into pain and all doors
to living seemed shut.

They held you like a window frame
where only looking was possible.
At the foot of the mountains

large plains where caribou roamed,
thousands of them – dotted like tiny tents –
busy on building strength just as yours had waned.

Only the mountain ice seemed to flicker in smile
as if it already knew that the low clouds curling down,
sounds of caribou, their snorts and swirls of breath,

hooves drumming the earth, the bones of them,
freckled chatter of the river nearby, cry of the sky
rumbling with intent, all these would channel you back

to health, that in the looking came the listening,
the opening of eye into self beyond self;
there too the beginning of new in old life.

# Mountain She

She said the mountain
had dreamed her, its
craggy eyes watching her
even when she was away
giving birth to an island
with her silver eyes.
That one day she became
a loom her breath weaving song
from the branches of birch
trees and the summer ridge
of flowers like a time born
before returned as skerries
and lattices of words hugging
the moon and sea.

# Dewdrop Days

Dewdrop days
when the weather
forecasts your eyes
and you first begin
a prayer, the garden
many hued, blackbirds
flitting about bright
eyed and astute,
a Druid's song from old
and you put together
your verse, a reindeer's
run that knows your lung
and she watching over
you, a land behind the
midnight sun, a voice
you hear in the rustle
of trees something
you are yet to know.

# The River Stone

Perhaps it was the stone that shifted things,
a nuance, tiny and yet more, as if the river
knew beforehand what might speak in her heart
and for the first time she'd hear something of other,
something below the surface, like a running
music score notes helped up by the promise
of more, flowerlets on the corridor of reasons
why, and so she sang birthed by the river,
by the stone of its smoothing, green and grey,
the moon in her eyes, ripples in her words.

# Afternoon Arrives

The afternoon drifting into evening, slow and
inexorable courted by insects in the humid
reach of the late hours, a time inevitably theirs.
He sees her pause, sketch book in her hand.
so many vibrations, she says, so much calling.

# Footsteps

I've followed you from afar, watching for your
footsteps to reach mine, or is it the other
way around, those first steps together
after so long, like the pink flush of dawn,
the beach stretching into light, dog roaming ahead?

Perhaps it's a daydream I've never 'owned'
yet which surfaces like a painter without
canvas making do with whatever else
is around? A summary with flourish.

Some days I hear your voice drifting
with the clouds and I'll say something
that the wind hugs and returns. I've
learned not to fold. Acceptance is such
a key to turn into more, a keeping

going when all else seems to have failed,
and yet the portal is another, the doorway
half moon, the faint flicker, like a tide
too tired to move.

# Green Stones

All the green stones on his desk
like a portfolio, comforting and strange,
different shades running through
them, dark, pinkish, white lines,
deep green so many dreams,
portals, sent by her from far
away, close to the bog lands,
the liquid light of dawn,
the farewell of dusk, and he
running into the sea, its wild
cold embrace, no surrender
just the ability to read the swirls
call out her name, be carried by the surf.

# Green Hill Days

The day cool, hints of sun and rain,
one of those when you're never quite
sure what to wear, and she with the
rainbow hands seeking to weave a song made
from the tongue of memory, like the lisp
of the sea stretching on to the beach,
and the green hills close by a hymn
of their own, calling you to be at peace.

# Birch Tree Loom

What it was to stand by the birch tree,
its slender limbs carrying the moon,
and you with your child's hands
reaching, trying to touch the branch,
me lifting you up that bit more?
How quiet you became, then laughing
and chattering, as if somewhere
within these moments we were both
carried home, at first just here, and then
more, as if another knowing had emerged
for which words would take their time.

Perhaps it was my grandmother's
lace curtains, her windows in Bideford
in North Devon, silvery and free
her apple tree the beginnings of song
for me, the last time of my seeing her
when I was four.

Perhaps too, the sea froth on the beach
caught on a piece of driftwood, bubbly
and trembling with the sea breeze.

Perhaps it was none of these or all,
a language of shimmer, silver,
puckering in the muted light.

# Forest Eye

You lying down on the forest floor,
listening to the language of leaves,
their faint flutter in the afternoon.

Was it you I saw elsewhere that day,
bursting into tears hugging that one
lone tree closer to the stream

its quiet and confident burble? I
wanted to lie down with you, close
me eyes, rest amongst all that's unsaid

and yet to be, something of the earth
and sky, the way a rainbow curves into
view and hope rides in for a passing hello.

# Canyon Song

High up on the canyon overlook
he sits flute in hand, as if framed
by white clouds.

Two ravens glide with the
currents, both shadows and not.

When a child, he had first
climbed the ancestor's trail
from the canyon floor to its rim,

the hand and footholds chipped
out of the canyon walls always
ready to be steps in the right direction.

# Own

What is it when you walk through the door of your own becoming and catch yourself thinking is this really me? And in your astonishment you stop or trip over your own foot, but hey is there any compulsion to keep walking or a fear that if you don't dwell awhile it may not be real? Experience is lived and not compiled. It's only after you might add to the description or become aware of the tiny follicles that adhere to whoever you are and wherever you step and go.

# The Dream Singing So

I wait for you in the tasselled light
of the new evening, like others
in the growing history of our
contact. What it is to be in love,
to yearn for the other, to be loved,
to love, to be loving, loving,
to cross the seas for her,
to drive across to the west
where the islands speak
with the clouds, to find
her waiting at the gate,
smiling, and then laughing?
Be in beauty, our Navajo
relatives say, be in beauty.

# In That Small Stone

an image of
a bird readying to fly.
She holds it close
even though she's
far away, a different land
where it's the escarpment
that is the song, her words
a lattice twirled by the sun
so that she has to get up
and dance, slow and rhythmic,
a point balancing between
the tenses, the summer's day,
winter no longer on the tip
of her tongue, the Old Ones
looking on.

# To Boundaries

What is it to walk to the boundaries
of your existence and say, I am here,
I am here and know you have arrived
at your true self after all this time,
and yet so soon?

# Years Then

In my mother's eyes tears never far
away, the windscreen of our lives.
Even now after all these years I miss
her smile. Mile after mile, the persuasion
loosens yet becomes the stronger, and
what you left behind keeps following.

# Paths

The breeze slight enough to quiver the water
pooled at the edge of chatter.

You still remember those words, old now
and yet afresh for you, as if you could
find a path through a forest by listening
to the breath of the day.

# Walking Clouds

The breeze calls you to find again the roots
of your being that marshalled your first steps
until you as the young boy knew to dance
light or walk strong as if a message bearer
from the clouds that always seemed to smile at you.

# Dropping Into Out of

Where the beginning path opens to itself
and you hear the rain on its way you
hesitate for just that moment too many,
and even though the rainbow smiles,
your shoes are immediately wet
and the only place to go is forward.
What then to be soaked, unprepared
and wondering? So that you close
your eyes and begin to sing, the deep
down yearning to be wild and real
or was it just that here lay the opportunity
to step out of what you'd thought so long
had to be you? And now the democracy
of rain said this is it no matter what you proclaim.

# Patched

The patchwork quilt of desire
roses in the vase, light peering
through the window, the war
chest of have-to's tucked inside,
memories that surface with eagle
eyes, and you with a shopping
bag full of poems yet to be written,
cow bell in the garden a yes to your
runaway smile, breeze a faint quiver,
the faintest touch, a long away choir
suddenly back past the breakers of the sky

# He Said Ever Since He Was a Boy

he knew he would be called to remember
things he shouldn't have to that he would
be good at that like a master of scripts. His
mother never chastised him. Rather her
presence was a gift in itself, bringing to what
she said a listening and at times, wonder. He
often thought of these words, how they could
carry the day. Listening was the key, as if by
way of invitation. Dance Dance till the moon
shouts and hoarse you speak no more. Then you will
hear what is given to you to hear. Your inner light
will bring you to a cave where the hoard is not
gold or emeralds but some stones. Do not be fooled.
Though they may look ordinary they hold the light
And will keep you safe. Listen to them. Listen
And be guided. The moon is calling.

# Cedar

She said the wood was cedar
that if you cupped it in both hands
it would smoke with its soft caress
a fragrance that would bring you
to the hearth of your longing
as if a canoe had carried you
to this exact spot this very moment.
Perhaps the rivers had brought the
first seeds and the earth stretched
to hold them. And now it reached
out to you as you the way dew
quivers on a leaf both here and yet not.

# River Tongue

She said the rivers are the tongues
of the earth. That's why there are
so many languages. That even where
rivers have dried up, memories linger
like pathways of the soul.

What was it then to kayak, to follow
the lines of a river, to know this one
more than that, rapids and eddies,
curves around rocks, the ease into smoothness,
large rocks looking on, story keepers, poems
edging into song, you with that scar
on your arm, pain turned into a hymn.

# River Light

You said some days memory gathers you up
and you learn to be quiet, listen to stillness
even as the past leans back into your life
and who you are is someone poised on
the edge of understanding, your intuition
the murmur of the river you loved, glint
of sunshine a calligraphy etched in light
and shimmer and in those moments
you return to the woman you have
now become.

# Tree Mosaics

Trees reflected in the river,
river reflected on the trees,
flickering shimmers, mirrors
to his eyes, he with the angel's
voice, trying to decide who
he may be, someone in-between,
yet one and the other.

# So Signed the Day

And you on the verge
of the mattress, firm
and soft writing down
the elements of the day,
your day, the rain trickling
stories as familiar as stone
and yet so different too,
until you stood outside,
soaking up the soak, you
said, shaking the moisture
from your hair, rushing back
in for a warm shower, your
body a cartography edged
by the earth, the valley
of the moons with its
ancient eyes softening
gaze yet inviting more.

# Otter Eyes

The path knows you before you set foot on it.
Perhaps it's been waiting and at last hears you
walking, your feet angled in the way you did,
both steady and edgy, the mountain ridge rich
with light, the flickering sunlight on the lake,
the feathered songs of birds, two otters on
the far bank, swimming towards your first words.

# Rainsome

The rain as soft as the faintest tickle.
I stand and lean against the old ruin
just where the damp fails to reach.
Though it is noon I can feel the moon
that will rise.

How you'd drum and sing for Brigid
and we'd circle the sky, spin songs
in three with poems as their ties.

What it was to love and be loved,
you and I twirling and laughing,
me with the antlered eyes.

What then the beginning of the look
away. Just as we got closer the weave
unwoven, something else entering
your fire,

The chalice you'd brought back
from Ireland, emptiness filling
desire and I moving away towards
The hillside, green without envy.

# Star Suite

Each night he sits by the window
as if edging into the dark.

Sometimes he hopes he'll see
a shooting star that will remind

him of her before she left. So many
years now he has held on to the

beat of her chest, how she created
wonder out of things few others could.

What it was the slipstream of her
imagination, different voyages

into being, her own trek, luminous
and wondering.

# Your Voice

You came to me
out of the clouds.
The sea stretching
across the bay
like rippling eyes,
your voice a Welsh tale,
stories combed up in your hair,
how smiles contain pain
as well as joy, the wind
a witness to all you've
desired and had to let go
yet even now the morning
wraps around you, carries
you that bit more, that bit higher.

# Water – In Praise of Desire

Water carrying the histories of life,
waves sparkling in the sun like
the silver lips of a dream, and you
stand and watch even after the wave
flattens into its own stillness.

I think of you like that, pain never
far from the surface, as if always
yet another question drifts towards
answers drifting past, the way you
liked to pat the surface of bathwater,
so many stories quivering just below
its surface of discovery.

# Word Skins

He seeks the skin of words,
to touch them if only for
the briefest moment, to be
moved in turn by history,
etymology, the beginning
sounds and meanings,
words in clusters, stretching
in different ways. He thinks
perhaps words are parachutes
you can float with. That you can
lean into a different sense of being,
a topography of suggestions, a map
of yearning and discovery.

# Your Music Dreaming

Your music wrapping around the day,
so that we lean towards each other
the whispered embrace of love,
the deep longing to be nowhere
else but here for true love
has no borders and yet too is a sanctuary
where language is more than a voice,
a journey like a river edging past
rocks sometimes sings to the clouds
the way you sang to your first born
and the eyes of the moon touched
you with the faintest glitter, and in
that moment you knew you had
become the person you always
wanted to be.

# Achill Island Stones

She and I on the island, furrows of memory in the land,
those taller standing stones, others, smaller  just
that bit away, onlookers and looked
upon too. She said sometimes you can hear
them talk, something faint, held by the breeze
both still and restless, reminding us that
paradox lies at the heart of creativity, that
at times people have said they saw them
move as if lifted by the arrival of dusk.
She added – perhaps stillness is another form of
movement, that stones were loyal
but not to be taken for granted, that
their gift was presence, that they knew
the movements of the stars and sun,
that maybe they were the original shamans.
Holding up the stars and the flickering light of dawn.

# Hebrides

What is it to lean across the land,
have it carry you further than you've
been, hopping across to other islands,
farewells and greetings, the weather
vane of reach and departure, history
in every quarter, a mountain reaching
up high above, songs that spring from
the earth, your eyes opened to sound,
music sweeping into inlets, a tidal seep
where you can push off the shore
hoist the sail of beauty, that you are
of here and not, but becoming so,
this and that twining in and out,
a weave that calls you into being
like a song running with waves,
running you home, home, home?

# Standing Stone

The lone standing stone, as ancient
as the breeze, leaning towards the earth
as if ready to embrace wonder, the one
and the other, calling down the moon,
calling up song, and us closing our eyes,
holding still, slight sway, the oaken dream
quivering in the water close by, an otherworldy
praise you can't replicate elsewhere, but
take in like the rainbow's edge of desire,
proof never needed, fields of green
murmuring their assent, us holding hands
as if folded in the loom of things.

# Walking Stone

His walk the everyday of existence, the small climb
up the hill, listening at the summit for the whispers
of the land, the stones that called in beauty,
the old cairn across the bay, a hymn to all that
shines no matter what's happening all round,

What then that day, clouds thick and unending,
plumes in the water, the old boat swamped more,
pains in his hand, the writing ebbing past, all
of that and less, the hero his dog walking ahead,
and he reminding himself, be with and not against,

allow the day its message, his voice the words
to choose, something more of the landscape,
words that dwell in the moist path of yearning,
ribcage of memory?

# The Portered Song

The portered song
as rich and thick as laziness
velvety on the sofa
and every bit a bed,
your eyelashes
holding the moon
and the night a wayfarer,
silken with cloud.

# Running Heart Fire

for Jon McClanahan, Navajo, Chinle, Arizona

I can see those horses running across the
plains of your sight, see them behind your smile,
the same smile that greets the dawn of each day
though your heart may be quiet at times
with the pain and unshed tears a man
cannot or feels he must not show.
I can see that you have seen your horse
run and fly with the Spirits of the departed.
That your eyes have seen
the skies of other shores.
I have heard in your smile
something of the hoof and early morning snort

of your four-legged one's fire
and love for life so great
that it would run to the sky.
I have seen that something of its own life now beats in my eyes
and the heart that sees you smile.

# Rippling

The day rippling into other just
as the weather forecast changed
and you raised your eyebrows
to all that was sailing past, no
microphone at hand, dream
wrapped by the sea, bare foot
testing the breeze, dog close,
breakers past the point, words
just that bit ahead. When you
reach out they reappear, close
and with different range, for
in the letting go is the letting in.

# At the Edge

I've come to the edge of living
as if a sharp bone were sticking
through the membranes of all
my words.

I can't see you unless I look
in different ways, as yet below
the surface of my eyes.

What then to step off beam,
to climb the clouds, be with
the earth and green surrounds,

to let go and challenge oneself
to be alive in all the contradictions,
no matter how it all seems, to have
being OK more than an act of survival?

# Her Green Eyes

*Se Suillean Uanie a'Thaice*

her green eyes
how her body quivered
when the sun fell into our lives
the first touch of dawn
the light that always found her
no matter how deep she swam
in the lake of her own dreaming
and him reaching for the drum
a Celtic whirl of vision
as rhythmic as the sun.

# Her Words Together

A rainbow's edge past desire,
listened to by the spider close
on the wall as if a portent
of all that she's wanted to say
but found too hard, boyfriend
running with the sea, her words
jumbled and refusing to be
at ease, until for enough
moments, she gives up trying
to get things right, to have
exactly the correct words
and watched the spider
draw from itself all it needed,
an alphabet of skills that held
together a tiny part of the world.
Perhaps there was a web in her
heart where words rested awaiting
her call, and she could relax into that,
a mosaic of chipped parts
of her life ready to get to work too.

# Echo Shore

You and I walking by the shoreline,
seagulls close by ready to fly, the tide
swirling in and between the seaweed stacks
that shape small coves and inlets of their own
like sentinels to all we can't see but intuit.

# Waiting

In the shadowed heat, humid
and moist, the crow waits, as
dark as expectations marooned.

In the cottage, she looks out
past the patterned glass. Everything
is still except for a line of sweat
trickling down her neck.

Across the bay, out near the breakers,
but closer than you think, he
picks up his binoculars, trains them
her way. She sees a faint flash

as the sun obliges, and she smiles.
They've been doing this for twenty
years. Only the crows have changed,
witnesses to sight.

# Breathing Light

Your words, dreams carried
by the marine fog. You wait,
patient as the moon, that edge
into dawn, brightening light,
tide uncoiling in the curve
of the bay, sentences like beads
of lace rippling on the tops
of waves.

# The Bay

The day still stretching into other,
the water almost laden with light,
and you remember when she dived
into the river wild and forgiving –
Even now you smile.

# Swedish Inlets

I wait by the edge of my understanding,
hoping the evening, with its cooler breeze
and softening of the light, will ease me
back into the world of the living, far
from the Sweden I loved, those many
inlets, cabins by the sea and lakes,
your stories and poems bobbing
across to me, mine to you, and for
those moments your pain would
diminish and our languages find
a way into the home of our loving.

# Notes Towards

The blue eyes of dusk, as if a gentle
goodbye, a turning inwards that slips
away as nonchalant as ever, and you
still, quiet and yielding, dawn and dusk
your favourite times, a musical score
you're yet to sing but on which you float,
a membrane of desire and withdrawal,
tidal and whispering, picked up by
the night and returned each morning
just as you wake, stars still in your heart.

# Sand Tremors

I wanted to write something fine
the way sand blown by a sudden
wind has a fine trail and tremor.
Perhaps in those moments, the
wind and tremor in the sand,
something of the holy makes
itself known.

# Elbow Light

The ribbed night, tree branches
singing, her voice a rainbow
as if climbing the stars, and all
the while the whispered breath
of the oncoming morning, dark,
purple, blue the first hints of yellow,
red and pink on the beach, dog
running back and forth, discovering
trails of scent even at that early hour
and he wanting reprieve from all
that darkened his thoughts, the loss
of her, empty champagne glasses
yet to be filled, photos alternately
taken down and put up again.
He tells himself that perhaps sunset
will bring resolution, the bookends
of his new life, and she inside
wiping down the kitchen table,
writing a new scale of singing.

# Lace

The day draped with lace, born of the sea
and its wild spray, and you out on the point,
singing songs into the breeze, as if lyrics
would carry you past all that held you back,
and for those moments you'd be like
a dolmen holding up the sky.

# The Road a Bridge

Between all you've desired and all
you have never known.

What is it to pass that way, to lean
out of the window of your living

and meet your expectations
coming the other way?

# A Poem Is a Window

A poem is a window
you can keep open or shut.

Perhaps it's also a lantern
when the days are dark

so you can see something
that otherwise you'd walk past

I remember her last poem
The one she wrote in-between

staying and leaving, a poem
that's a window to what was

and is not, yet remains like
a lantern in my heart.

# Beginning Light

Some days, this day, it is the shadow stretching from the mountain
that is the call to verse, your words lightening, lithe and potent
as you lean back into the beginning light, one step more away from sorrow.

# Windowed

All the windows open as if awaiting guests from all realms,
the sidhe and the leaves,

the patter of raindrops, last year's resolutions walking away
and the dog by the front

door, a guardian in the freckled evening the sun still up and
the horse-drawn cart

waiting for scheduling. Of course, it could all be different,
the sun set already, sky cloudless,

the dog scratching, and he with the flowers back from the
market ready to praise his wife.

But there's more, none of this is happening, just a fading
flicker of light on her desk,

words still scrambled and another coffee yet to be poured.
This time the dog's outside,

still watching for the postie who's already delivered the scant
mail, just a bill or two

and a card from a leftover sale sent by her sister three doors
away. It's that sort of place.

# Going

The day still, thick with memory,
She, gathering up her life, one
suitcase too many, the sorted
in turn becoming unsorted, books,
notes, folders, those favourite
cups with bright Mexican colours,
furniture left for others, clothes
to be carried, the rest discarded,
her first book almost her last,
and he arriving to help, pack
a little tighter, a minimalist she
once called him, essentialist
he replied that smile that could
carry her far, the dog by their feet,
names of stars still on her tongue,
the past fractured yet still hanging
together, the embraces between hope
and tears, he packing the final
pieces, door closed, stories still sleeping.

## The Rise

Where do I meet you now that you have gone away? Is it that you have eloped with the breeze, the first canter across the plains of your beginning, or the debris of twisted desires, the suffering in silence when the hands of abusers made your body theirs and hope lay in words you wouldn't have chosen yet which found you, reshaping calling to you the beauty that always seemed in your eyes the way morning mists hinted at surprise? You've gone down a path I can't follow though sometimes I think I see your footsteps in the sand on the beach, or that smile in the passing clouds we looked for omens in. Perhaps today it is the birch tree that is the choir and the seagulls messengers of relief. I know I'll sit by the fire and rest my head against you, the cottage door open just in case you returned, you a nomad who always found a way.

# The Shed

The shed, roof corrugated
silver paint faded, blistered,
rust the only ochre, the day
bright, the hot air glary,
shimmering in the faint breeze.

I sit apart, in the shade, recall
the first days, us as new arrivals,
Outer Harbor, then here at St Peters,
I the 'boy from Hong Kong',
seeking refuge away from
the ordered streets, bright
blue sky, straight lines,
a sky without clouds.

## Forest Walk

He follows where words take him,
sometimes to the lake, at others on
the narrow, curving path through
the forest, each step a wonder, even
after so many years.

Sometimes he hears words trailing
behind him, a slight catch on a fallen
branch, or where the stones talk to
themselves, and he stops to listen,
eyes closed, the better to see, to hear,

and waits a while, breath steady,
no need to rush, no need to know,
it's listening that is the verb, that
is the way to see.

# Memory

The ribbed edge of change, the day dreaming of more,
and you wait by the old stone cottage, no windows
left just the reminders of absence, the old path
overgrown, each year more indistinct, so that
you light a prayer stick offering its smoke
to the four quarters and to the memory
of memory where even silence has a note.

# River Singing

She looks across the frozen river,
listens for the shapes of words
amidst the creaks and groans,
turns back into her house,
the wood fire, warm and well
structured, a hymn of its own,
the bright woven fabrics from the
Costa Rica and Mexico of her
loving, places within her that
hold the light even as the days
shorten.

Sometimes she thinks the river
still moves much deeper even
though on the surface all is still.
But then she thinks everything
is moving often in ways she can't
see. Perhaps the dark is needed
so that ears will speak and meaning
take shape in the most unexpected ways.

# Bridge Sways

Where is the bridge
Now that your laces are undone?

What is it when you walk
and keep tripping over something
you let go, the way the full moon
holds the sky on the darkest nights
and our bodies become tides
and we might fight a mood

though it's the sun and moon
speaking, the trees reaching up
for one more dance with the wind,
you as a child painting the rainbow
you wanted to dance under and me
with the long walk over sand dunes
to find the surf and swirl too
dangerous, standing instead at
the edge of what might be, tracing
the currents hungry for more of a roar?

What then to be at the intersection
of yes and no and find in the body
of living a language that moves your
feet and toes, the clouds low, looking
for the elsewhere you thought you found
at the edge of a tongue of land?

# Webbed Will

I listen for the words,
carried by the Ancients
past the broken reminders
of original intent. What is it
there that smiles like the
jewels of the evening, how
the night dances on top
of water and small waves
and you wished you had
words that could slip in and
out of the light, that could
lean back into it and balance
into song or rest there like
woven light?

# Whispered Light

In the whispered light
thinner than memory
you dance, pale top,
red dress flicked with
silver, turquoise rings
something unsaid
waiting for an outlet,
you shimmer, liquid
and curved as if walking
in a mirage, lace swirls
of fingers touching
the sky, words floated
on clouds.

# The Wind As Song

Was it the breeze the brigantine,
nudging into the fabric of the day
like a mercenary wading through
shallows?

I waited for you up on the rise,
holding close my memories,
the walks by the river, love
making in the patches of sunlight
filtering  through breaks in the forest,
your blonde hair holding the sun,
smile like a rainbow, more steps
towards becoming closer
a couple in the making, just
like that, out of the nowhere
of living, carried by new stories.

# Words Up On High

How she sang, notes like eddies
in the river close by, the fortune
to open to sky, to allow words
to soar and topple, nothing
clearly defined, until the final
lines as if the moon were resting
on the hilltop and even the clouds
stretched for a better view.

# Forest Light

Sometimes I can still hear him
walking through the woods,
that little clicking sound he made
towards the end of his life as if
reminding himself that all that
he'd heard when younger was still
present amongst the trees as they
chatted to the wind and their neighbours.

Sometimes too, I have to sit down and
rest awhile as if to collect the light
emitted from the past. For all is living
even when decaying.

He'd devoted himself to that much,
the language of years, of light on
small pools of water, the dream
of dewdrops, the speckled white
of sudden cold.

# Her Hair

Braided with light and song,
glints of silver as if the moon
rested with her, so that even
on the darkest days when the
sun was low something sparkled
with her, at once far older
suddenly new, woven and lyrical.

# She Icelandic

In the crinkled light your words
shine through, born of the ice
and snow, carried by the tops
of birch trees as if they knew
each word inside and out.

I think of you like that,
your quest to be real,
to be at peace in the world
no matter how pain challenged
you otherwise.

I saw you once standing
in the snow when you
went out in search of
a comma to interrupt
the pace of your mind,

and you raised your
arms, hands tipped
by a pale blue light,
and I knew then you
were a woman of the rivers,
a swimmer in the depths
of meanings, and I knew
then all would be well.

# Inishbofin

Where the clouds gather, your home.
Is it you at the door everything ajar?

I wait by the shore looking up the
small rise, the path where hope once

walked and you'd smile that far away
smile that drifted across the bay.

The sea so blue today as if it too
remembered your first steps apart,

the elsewhere I never saw coming
but which keeps retuning, a tide

I can't hide from but immerse
myself in one more time.

# Quilted Sighs

The water's edge its lip lapping sound
periodic surges that you can anticipate
but never quite know when, that sudden
jolt or smacking sound.

Who is there when you open your mouth
like a gull squawking at the dawn you missed
and which returns somewhere in your bones
and though all apart you begin to feel at
home, the breeze quilting the water and you
with your sighs, with your sighs, your sighs?

# Edges

At the broken edges of light,
she waits for answers to
questions she hasn't quite
announced but which linger
deep within, a faint flutter
between knowing and not,
absence the path, familiar and yet apart.

She closes her eyes, listens to the sea's
tidal sighs, the swish and
lisping arrival of ocean
against the shore sweep
up the beach rhythmic
and ancient, so that she
begins to settle, her queries
held out to dry in the pale
sunlight of her living.

Only then the answers arrive –
in the squawk of gulls, the
runic patterns of their tracks
reminding her of him, his
sketches and chants, unassuming
gentle and wild. The day stretching
carrying his voice, reminding
her to keep going no matter what,
no matter what.

Perhaps, she thought, he had
become a bird flying with
the currents of air sweeping
into the words he loved,
nestling at the edges of sighs
edging over to the island
they both loved.

# Mountain Eyes

I've gone back to where the mountain
first spoke to me, its green folds and slopes,
gullies catching the breeze, rocks with their
unfailing gaze, sea further away, lapping
at the edges of memory.

I wait for you to join me, even though you're
far away in the Iceland of your choosing.
I sit for awhile running over the words I might
have chosen, a something else that keeps
returning as resolute as the tides, your
eyes so blue like a whispered sky bright
even in the dark that is night.

Perhaps today I'll find my way into
a poem carried by birds with their
feathered praise and the day will hold
gentle as your first words.

# Dreaming Sighs

Her face so open and quietly bright,
as if many years of stories rested
in her hands, an owl at night
watching over her because she
had done so much to maintain
the old ways where animals
and people were equal, birds too.

The land was different, varied.
Some places only shamans could
go, trailing stars from the deep
oceans of long ago lands.

When I saw her today she looked
at me with a smile that also
said: be gentle with the land as you
would with yourself. Offer
prayers to the smallest creatures
as well as the wide gaze of the sky.

Let your heart guide your way,
and dreams speak your truth.

# Akureyi Night

There are streets beyond the moon.
They reach deep down way below whatever you'd expect.
then reflect back what you've not yet said.

I want to visit this place
far from the madding crowd in my head.

But where I go so too do I.

House lights point across the fjord
poker-faced and straight, electronic
lines that touch the end of the photo
graphs of their own choosing.
We watched the sea ripple
a quiet surge towards the harbour.
There where you left your reindeer smile
and boarded again your past.

I am left over, forgotten by the sea's ebb and tide.

Fold over the photograph
one last time.

# Clothed in Rain

Out towards the furthest point,
a single light clothed in rain,
and in that moment the past
returned, a globe of its own,
both known and new, as if
familiarity were the keys
of a piano not quite in tune,
and yet enough for his voice
to be heard once more, and
though his wounds opened
again red with story, he felt no
fury and let silence be the language
dreaming, the sea speckled,
dog by his side, tide waiting.

# A Mheeky

Where are you now I can't see you
and yet know you're close by?
Is it the rain, its thin patter against
the window of your leaving, that
I must lean back against the sofa
and rest my head against your last
breaths, trying not to ask too much?
To let go even as I held on? Even
though I saw in your eyes the
coming of this day?

That last walk to the ancient cairn
in the Burren, Ireland, how you
clung on to me, my sighs as I walked,
scrambling to find my way. The day
so cold, moist and snowing, no drum
beat moments, the path followed
never a straight line but curving
in the Celtic swirl of beginning
and ending, of ending and beginning.
So that I left only a tiny piece of your hair
amongst the stones, away even from the cairn,
more sheltered and yet more open to the
lungs of the land, green and limestone
stretches and undulations of the bigger
picture your eyes always spoke of,
like a gentle band of light.

# Words Lining

Was it that words followed
or that they waited on a path
you hadn't yet imagined
but intuitively knew?
And that the first movement
was also the destination,
rock ledges where stories
gathered undisturbed by
a breeze?
Perhaps they were born
of the ancients and they
trusted you to shape
new understanding
while encouraging
that listening was
a portal between
one world and the other,
something more,
and yet a library too.

# Silent Plumes

She the winged dove carrying
poems from here to her beginnings,
the weight of years packed into
each memory, the hills stretching
into their deep green sighs and smiles,
the cove where she first swam,
and further away, closer to the light
of the moon, her first memories
of him, a sailor called to war,
whose only return was to her
heart, so that each day she planted
flowers, no matter how hard the effort,
nor how dark and moist the day.
Sometimes she thought she heard,
him calling out, and each year she
tried not to hear as she slipped into
the unbearable silence of absence,
beginning again and again.

## Without You

Without you I wouldn't be here. It's as simple as that.
I've been looking for you these last years, a wayfarer
carried by the moon in the stillness of a turning eye,
the last drops before dawn, the way grass shapes itself
to the sun, the memory of your first dog still strong,
tracks of loss across your face, the one shoulder
slightly dipped, the smile that gathered us up never
far from your lips.

I want to sit by the stones up on the ridge, a pathway
to meaning you can't gather by thinking, that you have
to stretch into, allow yourself to fall to be embraced,
the sea quiet today, no one else about, just, the reminders
of remainders, the tin whistle of yearning and memory,
tunes that ripple with the sun.

# Leaving is Arriving

Each time I arrive I think of leaving.
Perhaps it's a neurosis packaged
as other, a somewhere that'll be
more than another, more than before.
This time it's different, flowers in
your hair, body lithe and willing
like glints of sunshine in the
freckled face of dawn. I dance
to that now, steps an incantation,
sinuous and born of the coves,
gentle and vigorous, a tidal
breath and swell, and you
dive into the sea of meaning,
long stretches, movement
a beacon, a dream partnered
by soul.

# West Country

She said that when she was ill
the clouds helped her, how they'd
billow into the corners of her eyes
so that she could rest more, her pain
lessening. Perhaps the clouds were
her relatives from a far earlier time
when the first peoples moved into
this area, a place of green hills
and forests that spoke to her
in the movement of leaves
in the breeze. Everything
seemed to slow down yet
her thinking stretched beyond
what had become a daily lament.
One day she realised she could
talk to the clouds, sometimes
aloud, at others in that ancient
pathway of intuition, a knowing
beyond the expected, a pathway
of its own where solidarity was
the key and even at midnight
she'd hear songs drifting
across the landscapes of her
mind and she'd walk amongst
rocks and stones that some nights
reflected the memory of the sun.
it was there in the silence and patter
of words she began her healing,
a woman of strange and powerful eyes.

# Gone Away

I've come back to greet you,
the rosemary edging into
flower, purplish and nibbed,
like stars awaiting bees.

Where I look you've moved,
part framed by the window,
glimpses of more flowers,
like a passage home to a place
only you really know, the way
a deep gorge holds the history
of movement amidst settlement
and ancient bones become
the skies of innovation.
and story. And you in your
ability to traverse different
moments like the echoes
of dreams deep in the earth.

# How You've Moved

How you've moved
overseas, Sweden for
a new start, the writing you
always wanted to do, the way
words come together or head
off in different directions,
and you'd smile happy
with their independence,
the story of origins in each
word, pathways you'd say,
or words meeting up with
each other and becoming more.
Sometimes that was enough,
and you'd lean back, leave
things for a while, rummage
for sharp pointed sticks and twigs
to make runic the day. Sometimes
you'd cry as if tears were the language
of the moment, as you remember
those who've left your life or gone
quiet.

When I see a flock of birds skimming
across the bay I remember your smile,
your endeavour to understand,
be with the eyes of the day.

# The Borrowed Light of Age

creeping up, aches that don't
go away but persist in their
regard of you. What then to
find a trumpet player to blast
the pain with melody that's
unpredictable, soothing and
searching for those moments
that day unwinding, and every
thing changed and everything
stayed the same, the wheel turning that
one more time?

# Celtia

I was born here, the forest
with its green stretch into
being patched with light,
so that the language of trees
took root within me,
a reminder of the deep past,
the way new beginnings
are rarely straight lines
but curve into meaning.
Perhaps it was there,
so long ago, I first
sensed you, even though
you were so far away,
as if the breeze brought
new messages wrapped
in DNA, and the first
words formed on the lips
of our becoming, gentle
and knowing, written
and yet to be spoken.

# Singing Searching

I walk along the shore, looking for words
swept up on to the beach. Perhaps I will find
a story amongst the runic movements
of birds or there'll be something in the
sky calling for presence and new eyes.
I have learned to wait, to let patience
be the new song amidst the comradeship
of old piers, voices close to water, a flock
of dark birds overhead, migrating and
calling on their knowledge of so much
we don't see.

# Achill Ruins

Three-cottage corner the sharp
elbow end of hope, road twisting
onwards, emptiness the only
presence. I stop and look around
the ruins, mud-encrusted floors,
windows devoid of glass,
black-faced sheep that bunch up
and rush out when I step back.

It's nearing noon, but the sun
seems somewhere else. Perhaps
it's talking to one of the islands,
and the sea lifts to look around?

I pause, streaks of moss
on the walls, stillness
wrapping around, gathered
up at the old fireplace, usually
the last part to collapse, to
lay bare its soul. Today its voice
is resilience, silence its weave.
Perhaps too, there is strength in that.

# The Moon Filling

The full moon tonight with its eye
for questions, and you walking
along the shore watching the history
of breakers and quick surges up
the beach, thinking of him and
that other tide of separation.

# Word Splashes

She said words sometimes surfaced
from out of the river, glinting with sunlight
and the surprise of presence.

When that happened, whether
she stayed or moved, everything
was light, and though her words
thickened with intent, the river
with its sinuous prose always
found her voice, its murmur
the beginnings of thoughts
ancient and newly spoken,
like the riverbank listening
to the movements of the moon.

## At Then

Where is the holy when it is right
in front of you, and you pause,
breathe in and out, and light flickers
through the tall trees of your yearning?

# The Language of Skerries

The language of skerries, steep sides and mountain eyes.
The language of old still held by stone and sky.
Was it there you began your stories, ones on which
you could rest your head content with sea spray
and the beading of words? I know when I
think of you the two go together, the way
you wanted, the way you did.

# Evening Light

You lean against the gumtree, the river a thin embrace
of itself, a flickering dance past your sighs, and you
smile saying you are home again, home.

## Sounding Eyes

The breeze enough to quiver the water
pooled at the edge of chatter, the way
you still remember those words, old
now and yet fresh for you, as if you
could find a way through a forest
by listening to the breath of the day.

# Step Back To Step Forward

Don't wait for the sea to rise to brighten your eyes even if you
think you don't.

Perhaps it's the rays of a forgotten life that
peek through the forest of a long ago yearning,
a voice not quite heard but felt within the
membranes of your heart.

Perhaps too you were one of them, doing
all you would not do now yet which keeps
returning dulled and yet equally sharp.

What then the moment that breaks another?
The light that outshines other, the stream
rushing down the hillside quivering with
and yet sits on the rock of forgiveness,
poised in paradox?
Light, the eyes that see no matter what is thrown up,
drifts in from unwanted arcs
up.

# That First Voice

you still heed
even after so many years in
the cupboards of separation.
I think of you, your love of
estuaries and hill forts like
signatures of arrival and staying.

# The Light That Is More

The new moon, its thin arc
a window to the night, to what's
emerging, those words so long
on the tip of the tongue now
softly spoken in the generosity
of moonlight, her hand in his
gentle and warming, the tide
of their love carrying them,
carrying them.

# Bornesome

So many tasks, milestones, the forgotten words
of your grandmother returning on the
tide, a quiet lisp, before a burbling surge.

Was it you standing there, the river's
edge, waiting for the sea to stretch in,
sigh, that cycle for so long a mystery
and yet well known, sometimes awfully so?

Today the current is quickening,
a language of the moon, distance as
closeness, an ancient force and voice
of change, and I stretch to see further,
looking for your voice across the way,
something I can hold on to, even as
everything swirls and fades, the running
breath of stillness even on the shippiest
of days.

# Canyon Songs

Us in the Canyon de Chelly
holding hands as we walk,
pausing to look at the petroglyphs,
and pictographs on the canyon
images of red hands reaching
skywards, the old storage
bin too, moulded from so long ago,
high up: a difficult climb.

On the canyon overlook, a Navajo man
starts playing a flute, notes
carried by the wind as if he were
right in front of us, the sky blue,
breeze light. It's the day before
we leave the Poetry Retreat

and I'm feeling content and sad
at the same time. As is my want,
you remind me, and we smile.

What it is to walk in beauty,
to feel aligned with the sun
and moon, stars in a cave,
the old nudging the new?

Perhaps our lives are written
in the dust when the wind blows
hard and the tent trembles.

Or the young Navajo men
all wearing black as they
ride their horses through
through the washes and gulches
of the canyon and we close
our eyes and join in the prayer
of movement, the individual
songs that make us who are,
what we let go.

That day something shifted
in me, an opening to voice,
verse born of the earth, a young
Navajo boy laughing loudly
whenever he missed the football
I flicked towards him.

# Canyon Gate

Footpath Junction, Canyon De Chelly, Arizona

Each year I pitch my tent in the same place
not far from the gate by the tall, grizzled trees.

I like to be close to Dog Rock where the shamans come to pray.

Mornings I unzip my tent flap and watch the sun stretch
across the Canyon walls where pictographs and petroglyphs

look at us looking at them. At night horses come close
tell their stories with snorts and whinnies, hoof beats

like distant drums. Some nights I wake thinking it's raining
but it's only the cottonwoods chatting and chafing with the wind.

Everything is the same and everything is different.

Today Spider Rock, the home of Changing Woman,
the long, dusty, grinding drive, low gear thrusts through gulches

and washes, past hogans* and broken-down fences, then
the slippery steep climb through shale and loose rubble,

the day cool and sunny, shadows of two ravens circling,
until I touch the base of Spider Rock, lean into her embrace,

listen to the silence, the fullness of place.

* traditional Navajo homes, round and cone-shaped, door facing east

# Cathy Portas Card – no title, brightly yellow, blue and red

Once this land was open, a territory
of foraging where machines now drone
with percentage as the new currency.

Some days you stand there as if on the edge
of discovery hoping for more lines
to appear in the history of settlement
and movement.    Perhaps the footprints
of the ancients are found in the sky
and you have to let go of your
assumptions and listen to the clouds,
their shadows a verse of their own.

# River Dreams

Where the river pools before its
final stretch towards the sea
you think of the moon
bright lanterns in Hong Kong,
your mother's voice, sage
and rich with story, the way
hope bobs along on its own
journey, of being and letting
go and becoming more than
you imagined and yet
decidedly more you.

# Thirteen Borders

### 1

The wing with its many voices,
the day cold yet bright,

### 2

And you counting the three
hours  till the new start you
haven't yet announced.

### 3

The river curving back on itself,
me as a boy floating on a rubber
tube, sea edging close.

### 4

How I've longer to unpick the
scars of retreat, to be amongst
deep loving again.

### 5

What is it when silence sounds so loud,
after a long refrain you sail on?

### 6

The song of the sea that day, frothy
wake on the beach.

7

Your words drifting past, gathered
by the wind, then let go as if still
meant for me, following.

8

The clouds edged by the sun, the day angling
into other.

9

What it was then to peel an orange with a knife,
the rings of Saturn, the hoop of love?

10

I say the ocean carried the first songs that lie
deep within the Earth.

11

You run your hand across my forehead,
my scar the entry point for crystals
once embedded within rocks close to rivers
and shoals.

12

The gull flies sway seeking fish offshore,
joining others circling and dip into the bay.

## 13

Only the evening will cool, the sea a thin
blue, like liquid light rippling and lisping
into night.

# Walking Words

Sometimes the dream seeps through
the membrane of memory and what
once was a few lines becomes the
striations on the walls of abandoned
ruins as if the original inhabitants
were still present even though they
left long ago following pathways
we don't know but can intuit like
messages in the veins of our hands.

# Willowed

I've returned to the willows
where silence is no longer
a question and the breeze
is soft, the way a smile
broadens and becomes
more. Was it you who
walked by singing
from your toes,
both familiar and strange?